UNDERWEAR!

Mary Elise Monsell

pictures by
Lynn Munsinger

Albert Whitman & Company   Niles, Illinois

To Rich, David, and Derek, for their love and humor. **M.E.M.**
For Carla. **L.M.**

Library of Congress Cataloging-in-Publication Data

Monsell, Mary Elise.
Underwear!

Summary: Bismark the Buffalo is grumpy and
unlovable until his friends teach him how to
laugh and show him that wearing colorful underwear
can be great fun.
[1. Buffaloes—Fiction. 2. Grassland animals—
Fiction. 3. Underwear—Fiction] I. Munsinger,
Lynn, ill. II. Title.
PZ7.M7626Un 1988   [E]   87-25419
ISBN 0-8075-8308-1 (lib. bdg.)

Text © 1988 by Mary Elise Monsell
Illustrations © 1988 by Lynn Munsinger
Published in 1988 by Albert Whitman & Company, Niles, Illinois
Published simultaneously in Canada
by General Publishing, Limited, Toronto
Printed in U.S.A. All rights reserved.
10 9 8 7 6 5 4 3 2 1

Zachary Zebra did not like buttons or snaps or sleeves or slippers or zillions of zippers.

But he did like. . .

underwear.

He liked all kinds of underwear in all colors and prints and styles. His best friend, Orfo the Orangutan, loved underwear, too.

Every year Orfo took a barge from Borneo to see Zachary. Together they went to the World's Greatest Grassland Underwear Fair.

Each time Zachary and Orfo bought as much underwear as they possibly could.

They bought orange-spotted underwear and underwear with palm trees and bananas.

They bought zebra-striped underwear, leopard-spotted underwear, and underwear with fish and monkeys and kangaroos and elephants and colorful grassland flowers.

Zachary wore underwear with underwear on it.

Orfo wore underwear
with people on it.

Sometimes they wore their underwear all at once.

Not everyone thought underwear was fun. Bismark the Buffalo refused to like underwear. He was not a very happy buffalo. Bismark didn't smile or laugh or tell silly jokes.

And he certainly did not want to *wear* underwear, anywhere.

"Buffalo don't wear underwear!" bellowed Bismark.

"Underwear is fun," said Igor the Egret. He strutted on Bismark's back, happily popping bugs into his beak.

"Fun—ha!" boomed Bismark. "Buffalo don't need to have fun."

"*Everyone* needs to have fun," said Igor.

"Is underwear better than mudholes?" asked Bismark.

"Not quite," said Igor.

"Can you run faster in underwear?" asked Bismark.

"Hardly," said Igor.

"Can you eat underwear?" asked Bismark.

"I never have," said Igor.

"There!" yelled Bismark. "Underwear is useless!"

Meanwhile, Orfo and Zachary were having a great
deal of fun wearing all of their underwear. . .

everywhere they possibly could.

But Bismark grew grumpier and grumpier. In fact, he was SO GRUMPY that the bugs on his back flew off to find a nicer buffalo.

"Buffalo don't need bugs," thundered Bismark.

"I do," said the irked egret. He flew away to find another buffalo.

Bismark was all alone.

The grassland animals felt a little sorry for the gloomy buffalo.

"He's a sad case," said Orfo.

"He's good at finding grass," offered Zachary.

"But not good at keeping bugs," added Igor.

"It is a tragedy," said Zachary, "to be clever but not happy."

"He doesn't want to be happy," said Orfo.

"Or doesn't know how," sighed Igor, thinking about lost bugs.

"Buffalo don't need to be happy," snorted Bismark, who had wandered over to graze.

"Hmmm," said Zachary. Suddenly he had an idea. "Maybe you're right. I'll bet you can't laugh, even if you say the word *underwear* ten times."

"Buffalo don't laugh," said Bismark.

"There is a danger, of course," said Orfo. "You might not be able to stop laughing."

"Nonsense," said Bismark.

"You might be silly and tell jokes," warned Igor.

"I'll say it and I won't laugh," barked Bismark. "I won't be silly and I won't tell jokes and I won't have fun. I won't. I won't."

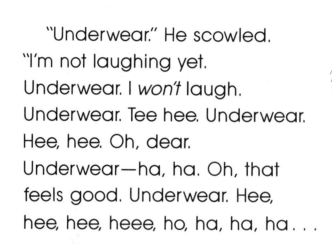

"Underwear." He scowled.
"I'm not laughing yet.
Underwear. I *won't* laugh.
Underwear. Tee hee. Underwear.
Hee, hee. Oh, dear.
Underwear—ha, ha. Oh, that
feels good. Underwear. Hee,
hee, hee, heee, ho, ha, ha, ha . . .

"Underwear. . .Giggle, snort. Ha, ha, ha, hee, hee, ho, hee, ha, ha, ha, ha, ha, ha, ha, ha, chortle, ha, ha, ha, ha. Underwear, **underwear, UNDERWEAR**! Ha, ha, ha, ha, ha, ha, ho, ho, ho, hee, hee, hee, hee, hee, hee. . ."

And try as he could, Bismark could not keep a straight face when he said the word *underwear.*

To this day, he laughs and tells silly buffalo jokes.

The bugs are back. Bismark is a cheerful friend whenever anyone is sad and lonely.

And, of course, old Bismark the Buffalo loves underwear as much as anyone.